TIGER HEAD

THE STORY OF THE 26th INDIAN DIVISION.

Arakan ★ Rangoon ★

The Naval & Military Press Ltd

Published by

The Naval & Military Press Ltd
Unit 5 Riverside, Brambleside
Bellbrook Industrial Estate
Uckfield, East Sussex
TN22 1QQ England

Tel: +44 (0)1825 749494

www.naval-military-press.com

In reprinting in facsimile from the original, any imperfections are inevitably reproduced and the quality may fall short of modern type and cartographic standards.

UNITS which served with the DIVISION during the period JULY 1942 to MAY 1945

BRIGADES
4th Indian Infantry Brigade. 36th Indian Infantry Brigade. 71st Indian Infantry Brigade.

ARMOUR
25th Dragoons. 146th Regiment Royal Armoured Corps.

ARTILLERY

Royal Artillery
8th Field Regiment. 160th Field Regiment. 6th Medium Regiment. 36th Light A. A. Regiment.

Indian Artillery
3rd, 7th and 27th Indian Field Regiments. 1st Indian A. A. Anti-Tank Regiment. 20th Indian Mountain Regiment.

ENGINEERS
28th, 72nd and 98th Indian Field Companies. I.E. 328th Indian Field Park Company. I. E.

SIGNALS
Royal Corps of Signals. Indian Signal Corps.

INFANTRY

British
1st Battalion Warwickshire Regiment. 1st Battalion Lincolnshire Regiment. 2nd Battalion Green Howards. 1st Battalion Wiltshire Regiment. 1st Battalion North Staffordshire Regiment.

Indian
5/1st Punjab Regiment. 6/6th Rajputana Rifles. 2/7th Rajput Regiment. 8/8th Punjab Regiment. 5/9th Jat Regiment. 6/11th Sikh Regiment. 12/12th Frontier Force Regiment. (Machine Gun Battalion.) 14/13th Frontier Force Regiment. 2/13th Frontier Force Rifles. 8/13th Frontier Force Rifles. 7/15th Punjab Regiment. 9/15th Punjab Regiment. 5/16th Punjab Regiment. 7/16th Punjab Regiment. 1/8th Gurkha Rifles. 3/9th Gurkha Rifles. 1/18th Royal Garhwal Rifles. 5/18th Royal Garhwal Rifles. 2nd Ajmer Regiment.

SERVICE CORPS
Royal Indian Army Service Corps.

MEDICAL
Royal Army Medical Corps. Indian Army Medical Corps.

ORDNANCE
ELECTRICAL & MECHANICAL ENGINEERS
PROVOST
POSTAL
MISCELLANEOUS
41st Indian Beach Group.

THE VICTORIA CROSS

Major FERGUSON HOEY, 1st Battalion, the Lincolnshire Regiment.
On FEBRUARY 16th 1944, Major Hoey's Company was part of a force ordered to take a feature near NGAKYEDAUK at all costs.

After a night march through enemy-held positions Major HOEY personally led his men right up to the objective under heavy M. G. and rifle fire from the front and flank. Although badly wounded, Major HOEY never faltered and reached the objective, where he killed all the occupants of the strong-point before he himself fell mortally wounded.

His leadership was unexampled and his complete disregard of personal danger was the inspiration which carried his depleted Company to the objective.

HAVILDAR UMRAO SINGH. INDIAN ARTILLERY.

When his gun position was repeatedly attacked in the Kaladan Valley, Hav. Umrao Singh inspired his detachment to beat off the assault. Though twice wounded he held off three more attacks. All his men but two, were killed or wounded. When the final onslaught came, Hav. Umrao Singh seized a gun bearer and closed with the enemy. He struck down three Japs in desperate efforts to save his gun and after furious hand-to-hand fighting was knocked senseless. He was eventually found beside his gun, severely wounded, and surrounded by ten dead Japs.

BATTLE CASUALTIES. Consolidated Figures for 1944

Forn/Unit.	Killed				Wounded				Missing			
	Offrs.	VCOs.	O Rs.	NCsE.	Offrs.	VCOs.	O Rs.	NCsE.	Offrs.	VCOs.	O Rs.	NCsE.
36 Bde. HQ	0	0	1	0	1	0	2	0	0	0	0	0
71 Bde. HQ	0	0	0	0	1	0	0	0	0	0	0	0
Artillery.	4	0	16	0	8	0	48	0	0	0	0	0
Engineers.	0	0	3	0	1	0	15	0	0	0	0	0
Infantry.	19	10	443	1	38	37	1,492	3	3	0	92	5
MG Bn.	1	0	0	0	0	0	0	0	0	0	0	0
Signals.	1	0	3	0	1	1	3	2	0	0	0	0
Medical.	0	0	1	0	0	0	7	1	0	0	0	0
RIASC.	0	0	0	0	0	0	3	0	0	0	0	0

INDIAN ARMY ORDNANCE CORPS

INDIAN ELECTRICAL AND MECHANICAL ENGINEERS

INDIAN PROVOST CORPS

ROYAL ARMY MEDICAL CORPS

ROYAL INDIAN ARMY SERVICE CORPS

2nd AJMER REGIMENT

11th SIKH REGIMENT

12th FRONTIER FORCE REGIMENT

UNITS which served during the period JU

BRIGADES
4th Indian Infantry Brigade. 36th Indian Infantry Brigade. 71st Indian Infantry Brigade.

ARMOUR
25th Dragoons. 146th Regiment Royal Armoured Corps.

ARTILLERY

Royal Artillery
8th Field Regiment. 160th Field Regiment. 6th Medium Regiment. 36th Light A. A. Regiment.

Indian Artillery
3rd, 7th and 27th Indian Field Regiments. 1st Indian A. A. Anti-Tank Regiment. 30th Indian Mountain Regiment.

ENGINEERS
28th, 72nd and 98th Indian Field Companies. I.E. 328th Indian Field Park Company. I. E.

SIGNALS
Royal Corps of Signals. Indian Signal Corps.

INFANTRY

British
1st Battalion Warwickshire Regiment. 1st Battalion Lincolnshire Regiment. 2nd Battalion Green Howards. 1st Battalion

 **25th DRAGOONS** **146th Regt. ROYAL ARMOURED CORPS**

with the DIVISION
LY 1942 to MAY 1945

Wiltshire Regiment. 1st Battalion North Staffordshire Regiment.

Indian
5/1st Punjab Regiment. 6/6th Rajputana Rifles. 2/7th Rajput Regiment. 8/8th Punjab Regiment. 5/9th Jat Regiment. 6/11th Sikh Regiment. 12/12th Frontier Force Regiment. (Machine Gun Battalion) 14/12th Frontier Force Regiment. 2/13th Frontier Force Rifles. 8/13th Frontier Force Rifles. 7/15th Punjab Regiment. 9/15th Punjab Regiment. 5/16th Punjab Regiment. 7/16th Punjab Regiment. 1/8th Gurkha Rifles. 3/9th Gurkha Rifles. 1/18th Royal Garhwal Rifles. 5/18th Royal Garhwal Rifles. 2nd Ajmer Regiment.

SERVICE CORPS
Royal Indian Army Service Corps.

MEDICAL
Royal Army Medical Corps. Indian Army Medical Corps.

ORDNANCE
ELECTRICAL & MECHANICAL ENGINEERS
PROVOST
POSTAL
MISCELLANEOUS
41st Indian Beach Group.

ROYAL ARTILLERY

INDIAN ARTILLERY

INDIAN ENGINEERS

ROYAL CORPS OF SIGNALS

INDIAN SIGNAL CORPS

LINCOLNSHIRE REGIMENT

12th FRONTIER FORCE REGIMENT

13th FRONTIER FORCE RIFLES

9th JAT REGIMENT

7th RAJPUT REGIMENT

6th RAJPUTANA RIFLES

16th PUNJAB REGIMENT

THE VICTO

Major FERGUSON HOEY, 1st Battalion, the Lincolnshire Regiment. On FEBRUARY 16th 1944, Major Hoey's Company was part of a force ordered to take a feature near NGAKYEDAUK at all costs.

After a night march through enemy-held positions Major HOEY personally led his men right up to the objective under heavy M. G. and rifle fire from the front and flank. Although badly wounded, Major HOEY never faltered and reached the objective, where he killed all the occupants of the strong-point before he himself fell mortally wounded.

His leadership was unexampled and his complete disregard of personal danger was the inspiration which carried his depleted Company to the objective.

HAVILDAR UM

* * * *

BATTLE CASUALTIES. Co

Fmn/Unit.	Killed				Offrs.
	Offrs.	VCOs.	O Rs.	NCsE.	
36 Bde. HQ	0	0	1	0	1
71 Bde. HQ	0	0	0	0	1
Artillery.	4	0	16	0	8
Engineers.	0	0	3	0	1
Infantry.	19	10	443	1	38
MG Bn.	1	0	0	0	0
Signals.	1	0	3	0	1
Medical.	0	0	1	0	0
RIASC.	0	0	0	0	0

15th PUNJAB REGIMENT

8th PUNJAB REGIMENT

...RIA CROSS

HAVILDAR UMRAO SINGH, INDIAN ARTILLERY.

When his gun position was repeatedly attacked in the Kaladan Valley, Hav. Umrao Singh inspired his detachment to beat off the assault. Though twice wounded he held off three more attacks. All his men but two, were killed or wounded. When the final onslaught came, Hav. Umrao Singh seized a gun bearer and closed with the enemy. He struck down three Japs in desperate efforts to save his gun and after furious hand-to-hand fighting was knocked senseless. He was eventually found beside his gun, severely wounded, and surrounded by ten dead Japs.

...RAO SINGH.

* * * *

...nsolidated Figures for 1944

Wounded			Missing			
VCOs.	O Rs.	NCsE.	Offrs.	VCOs.	O Rs.	NCsE.
0	2	0	0	0	0	0
0	0	0	0	0	0	0
0	48	0	0	0	0	0
0	15	0	0	0	0	0
37	1,492	3	3	0	92	5
0	0	0	0	0	0	0
1	3	2	0	0	0	0
0	7	1	0	0	0	0
0	3	0	0	0	0	0

LINCOLNSHIRE REGIMENT

NORTH STAFFORDSHIRE REGIMENT

WILTSHIRE REGIMENT

GREEN HOWARDS

ROYAL WARWICKSHIRE REGIMENT

1st PUNJAB REGIMENT

18th ROYAL GARHWAL RIFLES

9th GURKHA RIFLES

8th GURKHA RIFLES

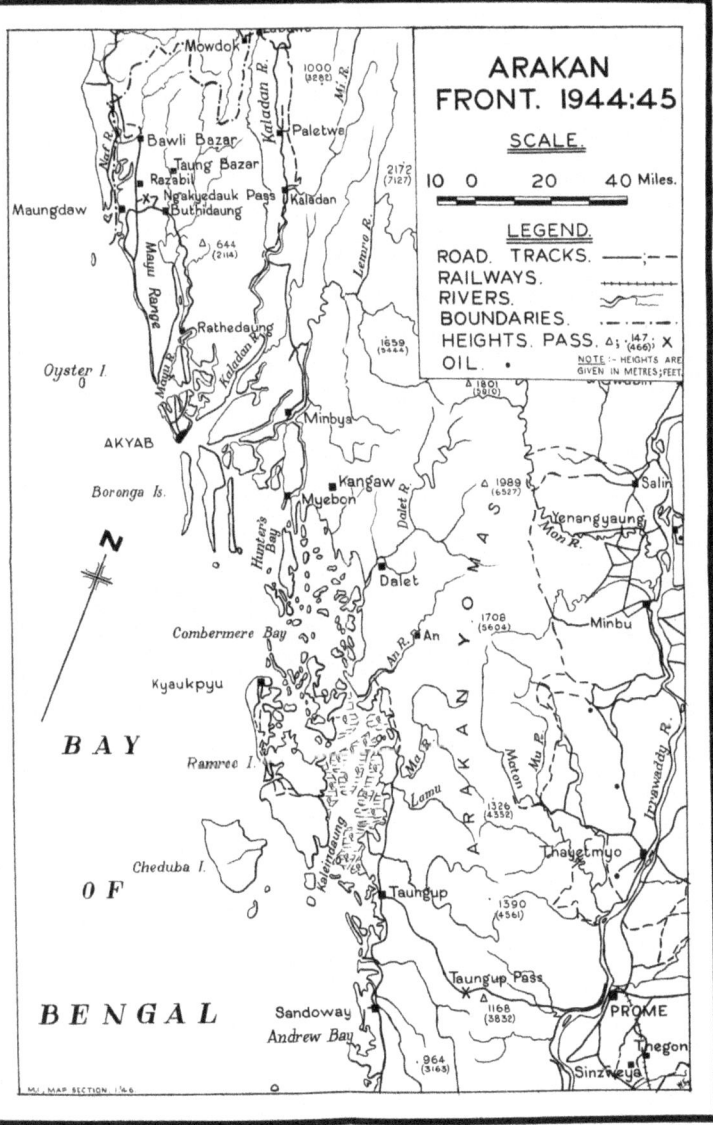

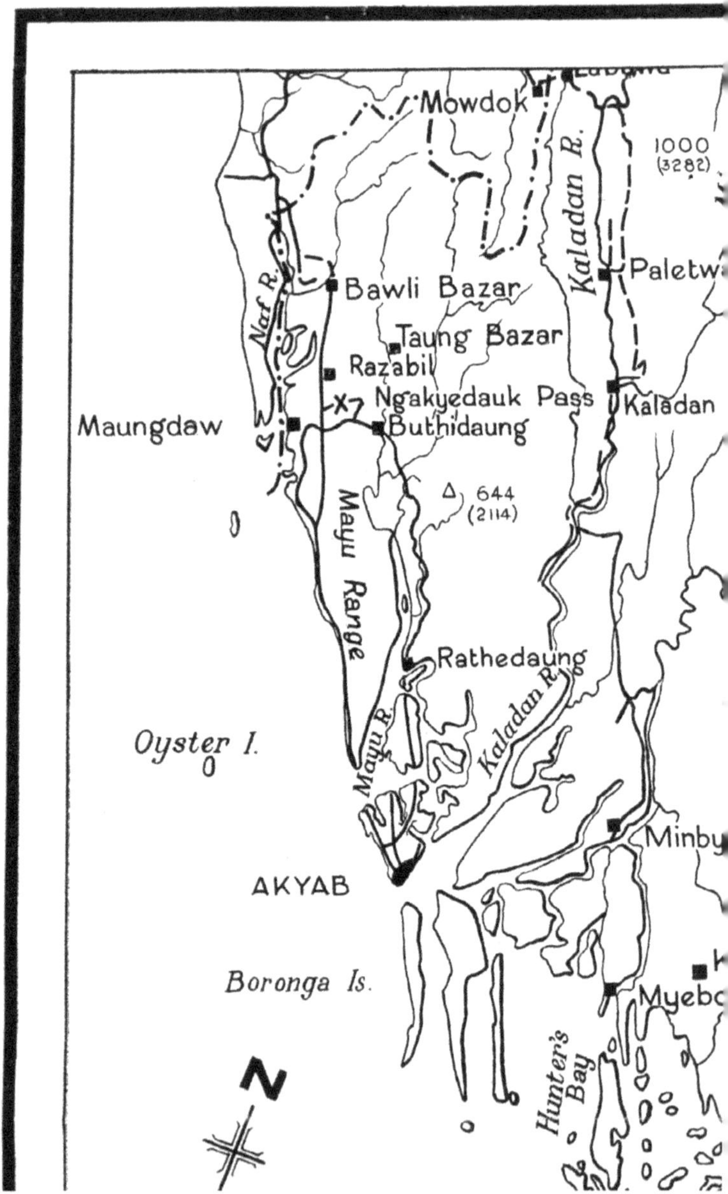

Mowdok
Kaladan R.
1000
(3282)
Paletw
Naf R.
Bawli Bazar
Taung Bazar
Razabil
Ngakyedauk Pass
Kaladan
Maungdaw
Buthidaung
644
(2114)
Mayu Range
Rathedaung
Kaladan R.
Mayu R.
Oyster I.
Minby
AKYAB
Boronga Is.
Myebo
Hunter's Bay
N

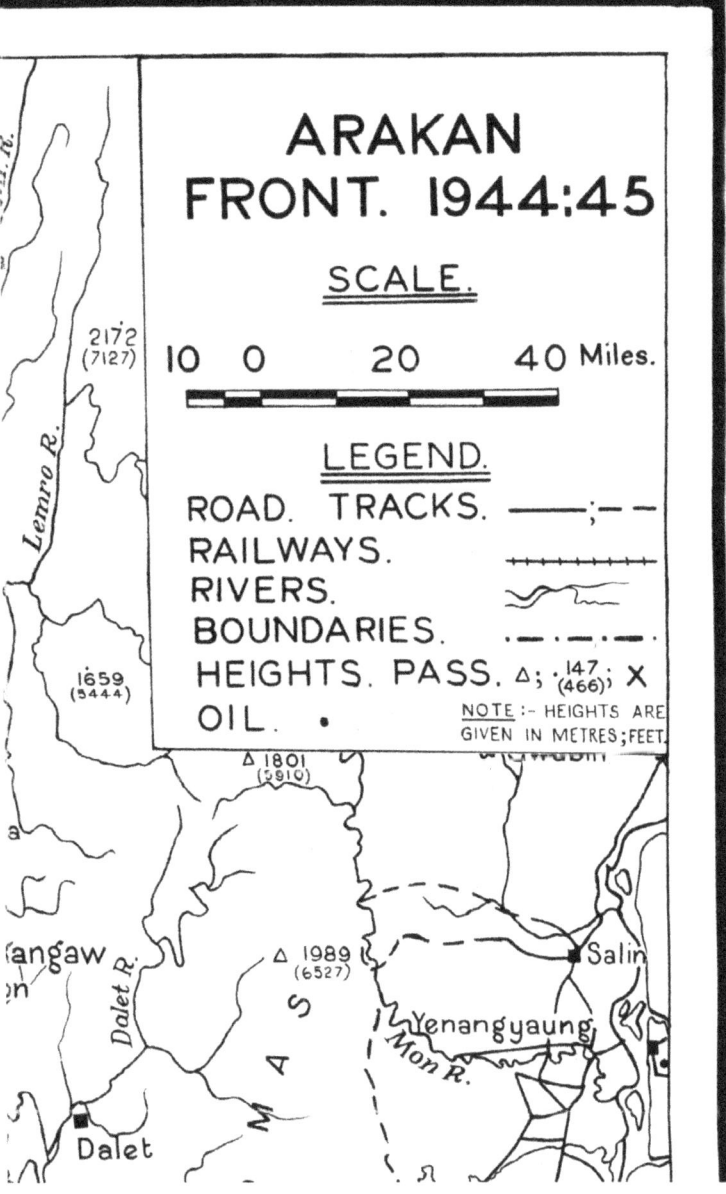

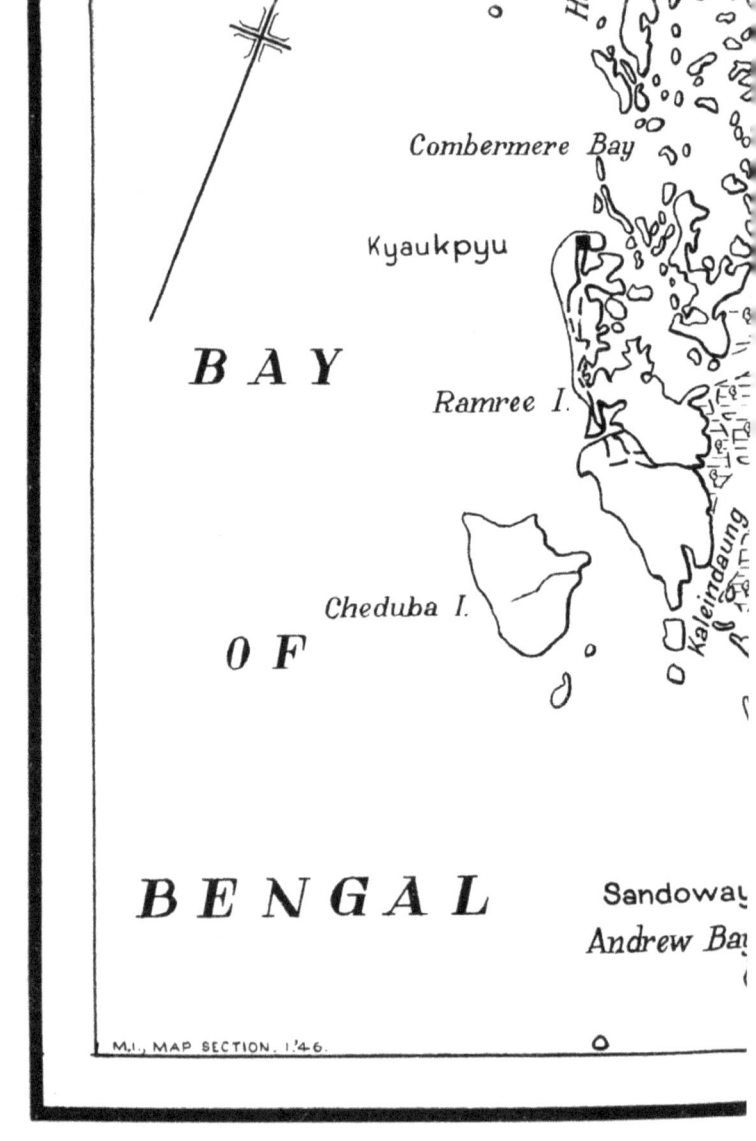

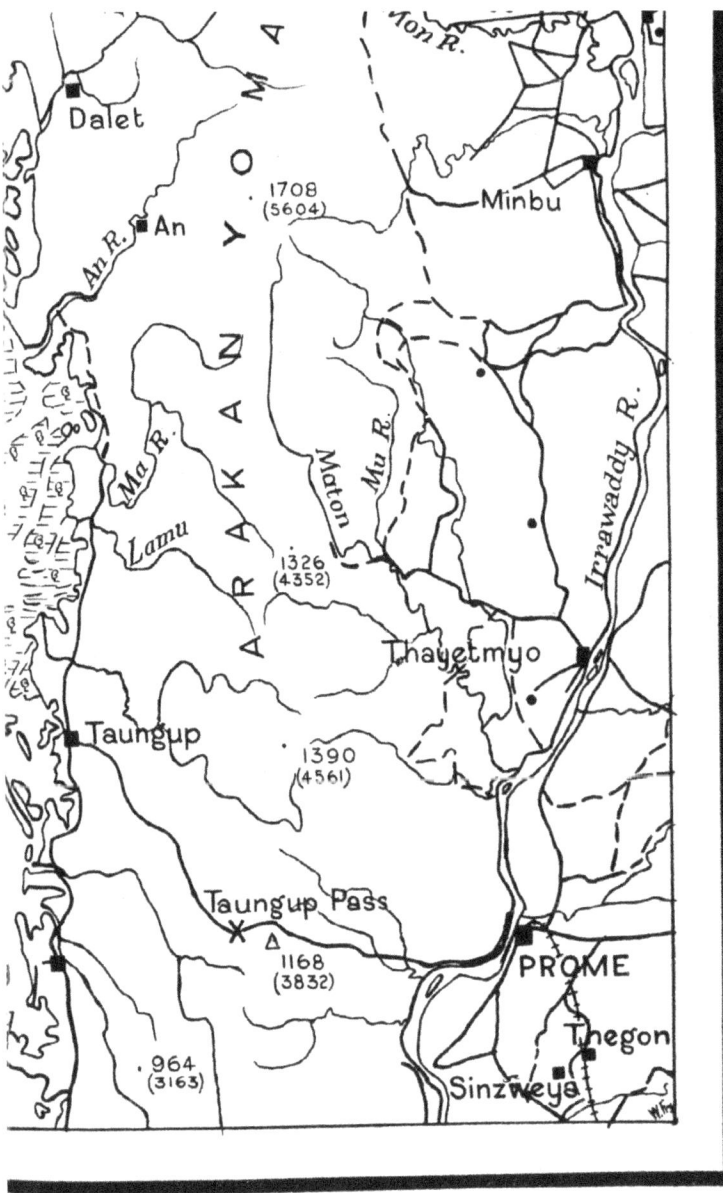

BRIGADE COMMANDERS

4th Indian Infantry Brigade
1. Brig. A. W. Lowther, C.B.E., D.S.O., 29th March, '43—18th Jan. '45.
2. Brig. J.F.R. Forman, C.B.E., D.S.O., from 19th January '45.

36th Indian Infantry Brigade
3. Brig. K. S. Thimayya, D.S.O., (left) 1st April—31st Aug. '45. (Brig. I.C.A. Lauder from 23rd April—8th June, '45).

71st Indian Infantry Brigade
4. Brig. R. C. Cottrell-Hill, D.S.O., O.B.E., M.C., 28th January, '44—28th February, '45.
5. Brig. H.P.L. Hutchinson, from 1st April, '45.

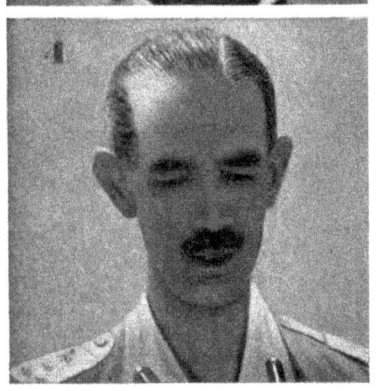

Maj. Gen. C.E.N. LOMAX, C.B., C.B.E., D.S.O., M.C., commanded the division from April 1943 to April 1945.

Maj. Gen. H.M. CHAMBERS succeeded to the command in April 1945.

HILL 1070

TIGER HEAD
Part I—The Arakan.

VETERANS of the Burma campaign—and more especially of the Arakan—are men of the 26th Indian ("Tiger Head") Division. To this Division so feared by the Japs that Tokyo radio specifically referred to it as the "famous" Tiger Head Division goes the credit for holding our monsoon line in the Arakan for two seasons, twice stabilising a situation which threatened danger to our forces, and finally as the crown for this arduous thankless campaigning over two years of war, the triumphant entry into Burma's capital Rangoon after a swift succession of leapfrog landings down the coast.

The 1942-43 Burma campaign when we forced the Japs down to their Akyab defence line at Donbaik to learn to our cost that we were not yet past masters at the art of jungle war, war coming to its unhappy conclusion in encirclement and withdrawal when the "Tiger Head" Division first raised its standard in the battlefield.

To the aid of the withdrawing weary elements of the Fourteenth Indian Division, went the 26th Indian Division.

In January of that year the Division was fighting over the

ground south of the Maungdaw-Buthidaung road and east of the ridge in the Kalapanzin valley which it was later to know so well. By May, the Division under the leadership of Major General C.E.N. Lomax, who had taken over command a month before, had stabilised the Arakan front. At one time during this period of scattered action the Divisional commander had not only his own three brigades to handle, but three others as well.

Jungle war was not the science it is today. As a theatre of war the Arakan had always exhibited features of uncompromising difficulty in regard to lines of communication and in those early days the situation was at its primitive worst.

But in spite of that the "Tiger Head" Division, displaying early the tenacity which was to be its outstanding feature, held on to our monsoon line. Not only did it control west Mayu, but the Teknaf peninsular as well—the neck of land jutting out to the north of the Naf river estuary. Here there was reckoned to be always a danger of a Japanese landing which would give him quick access to our line of communication from Cox's Bazar to Bawli. And more than this, the Division were patrolling east of the Mayu in the flooded paddy of the Kalapanzin valley and south from Goppe and Taung Bazars. To Goppe then ran only a mule track over the mountains—every yard during the monsoon a hardship to man and beast.

The Lincolns—crack British regiment of this Division who were to take part finally in the Rangoon landings—even at this early stage evinced their qualities in battle. Their's was the raiding exploit on Maungdaw then in Jap hands, where daring and improvisation hand in hand, convinced the Jap that the Allied forces still had tough fighting qualities. Not only could the "Tiger Heads" hold but they could also strike—how swiftly, critical events of the Spring of 1944 were to show.

In the Arakan cockpit then, the 26th Indian Division held the Jap and prevented him at that early stage from exploiting his initial advantage and pressing us further back towards the vital port of Chittagong and the plains of Bengal.

This was their task until, in the late autumn of 1943, the 7th Indian Division fresh from the jungle training schools of India began to move in to their relief.

Winter 1943-44 for the 26th Indian Division was to be a period of resting and training but still with an operational commitment. From the Kaladan valley running parallel to the Kalapanzin on the east, a Jap threat existed. At the end of the valley at Mowdok where the Indo-Burma border ran, was a gateway into India. One of the "Tiger Head's" battalions was given the task of controlling this gateway.

In the Spring of 1944 the pressure advance down West Mayu culminating with the capture of Maungdaw by the 5th Indian Division, the building of the Ngakyedauk Pass and the opening of the new phase of an advance on a two Division front with the Seventh Indian Division all east of the Mayu ridge, unfolded a new battle picture.

To this threat the Jap reacted with a stepped-up instalment of his long-planned counter-offensive into India which dominated the entire Burma battlefield from early February to the end of June 1944.

The invasion forces of Tanabashi swept up the fringe of the Arakan Yomas and into Taung Bazar, the Ngakyedauk Pass was cut, the advance on Buthidaung was halted, and 7th Indian Division Headquarters moved back into the " Admin. Box" at the foot of the Ngakyedauk Pass, to fight their never to be forgotten " no surrender " battle which taught the Jap, for the first time, our ability to stand and fight.

The situation in the Arakan to the outside world was critical. But in the Fourteenth Army this counter-offensive had been anticipated and it was not for nothing that the " Tiger Head " Division was waiting north of Chittagong.

For the second time they were called upon to restore the situation in the Arakan. The Division marched to meet the new Jap challenge as it had marched to meet the first. A record road and rail move was made and within forty eight hours of leaving Chittagong, the leading brigade of the Division was in action after travelling well over a hundred miles.

Two battalions of the advance brigade, one of them a battalion of the 1st Punjab Regiment, temporarily came under command of the Fifth Indian Division which had already begun to force a way into the Ngakyedauk Pass (Okeydoke Pass of later familiarity) to relieve the Seventh Indian Division, whose H.Q. were fighting in their famous " Admin. Box ".

The reopening of the pass, which the Japs had held closed for 16 days from February 7th to 23rd, with the historic meeting of Punjabi infantry from the relieving force and Scottish troops from the Seventh Indian Division, is an epic in itself. The clearing of the notorious Hill 1070, vital to the freeing of the pass, was accomplished with remarkable speed considering the strength of the Japs' fortress posts.

The ubiquitous Lincolns, third battalion of the " Tiger Head " Division's advance brigade, had meanwhile crossed the Goppe Pass and recaptured Taung Bazar, and three battalions from another brigade, including 2/7th Rajputs and Wiltshires, followed quickly, under orders to bear down southwards in the Kalapanzin valley and to link up with 7th Indian Division in the area of Sinzweya.

The 26th now had four battalions east of the Mayu Ridge. All were on a pack basis without gunners in support. An Indian mountain regiment came in later.

A serious situation had developed in the Briasco Bridge and Maunghnama areas where the Japs, after crossing the Mayu Ridge, had established road blocks on the main road from Bawli to Maungdaw and become a general nuisance to supplies and transport. 36th Indian Infantry Brigade of 26th Indian Division—was called on to meet this threat, and completely removed it. A Punjabi battalion pursued and cleared the enemy from the ghastly jungle country on one of the highest and steepest parts of the Mayu Ridge.

The battle of the Arakan was reaching its climax and the " Tiger Head " Division was in the thick of it. Fighting, patrolling and mopping-up was ceaseless, but after an Indian battalion and the Wiltshires had won a bloody engagement on a hill feature known as " Wing," the end of this critical phase came in sight with a glorious exploit by Major Ferguson Hoey of the Lincolns, who took Point 315, overlooking the " Admin Box " itself. Major Hoey was killed in winning the V.C.

With Ngakyedauk Pass cleared and the " Admin. Box " relieved, the Jap bid to reach India the Arakan way had been smashed. Troops of the 26th Indian Division had taken a leading part, but further tasks lay ahead.

By now the heat and humidity of the Arakan spring was beginning to tell. Dust was flying in ever-increasing clouds, water was scarce, and with the heat so oppressive most of our moves were completed in early morning or by moonlight.

The red danger light was now flickering from the Imphal

plain where 4th Corps troops were being surrounded in the state of Manipur and the troops who had fought the earlier battle of the Arakan were called upon to reinforce the garrison and assist in breaking the Japanese ring, while on west Mayu the 25th Indian Division relieved the Fifth. On East Mayu the "Tiger Head" Division took over from the Seventh. Buthidaung had been captured and the position east of the Kalapanzin stabilised but stern fighting still lay ahead of Gen. Lomax' men.

Shortly before the relief, 7th and 26th Indian Divisions again united in beating the Japanese when a party of 400 Japs staged a suicide assault on the "Admin Box" and Divisional headquarters once more found itself manning slit trenches on a perimeter. From inside the "box" Seventh Division troops held back this raiding force, while the Lincolns and the Garhwalis of the "Tiger Head" Division—a proved battle partnership—beat up the remnants between the "chota box" and the Maungdaw-Buthidaung road.

Round Buthidaung there was still stern fighting where one Brigade Headquarters found itself occupying an area not a hundred yards from that it had used a year before while men of the Frontier Force Rifles were clinging to positions on the tip of enemy-occupied "East Finger" and being supplied at night by jawans of the battalion playing tag with Jap patrols.

Down here too, the Lincolns were in action again with the support of tanks of the 25th Dragoons against two features known as "Spit and Polish." Here the Jap was well dug in and displaying his old tenacity in positions which menaced our communications. Enemy dead counted in the field after this action numbered 140. A battalion of 16th Punjabs who took the positions over from the Lincolns held them against repeated counter-attacks.

But most memorable and bitter was the battle for Point 551 south of the Maungdaw-Buthidaung road in what is generally described as the "tunnels" area. This feature was vital to the control of the Maungdaw-Buthidaung road and the completion of the Fourteenth Army's spring tasks.

Point 551 juts out of the tangle of foothills on the eastern side of the Mayu ridge. Its steep slopes were formidable, the approaches to them difficult. A determined Jap garrison could from this peak defy artillery concentrations and dislodgment.

But to this attack the "Tiger Head" division brought a greater measure of determination. The whole job took them three weeks. In the early morning of May 3rd the position finally fell to men of the 2/7th Rajputs and more than 150 dead Japs were counted in the area, and many more must have been buried by the shelling of the massed Divisional artillery.

The monsoon was approaching and the time came to withdraw to the planned monsoon line. As part of this

LINCOLNS AND GARHWALIS CLEAR UP IN THE "CHOTA BOX".

plan Buthidaung had to be evacuated and the Kalapanzin valley south of Taung Bazar abandoned.

But there was to be a final battle before the rain curtain of the monsoon came down on the last act of the Arakan battles of ' 44. West and south-west of Buthidaung a battalion of Japs intruded into a gap between two " Tiger Head " battalions. They attacked a brigade headquarters and a battery of the Division's jungle field regiment.

But Indian and British troops were more than a match for his audacious valour. They closed in on the intruder from both sides to squeeze him to death. Throughout the hot afternoon both sides fought savagely until the Japs were wiped out. The tank men of the 25th Dragoons who were in the action too reported that never had they seen such a concentration of Japs in a small area. With all their ammunition expended they were literally crushing the Jap to death under their grinding tracks. Four hundred Japs perished in that vain bid for last minute glory and advantage. It was about this time that the Tokyo radio commenced to refer to the famous " Tiger Head " Division—news of the valour of this veteran formation had filtered apparently through the screen of censorship and deceit which shielded the Japanese homeland from the truth about the ability of the opponents of the Imperial Nipponese Army.

This last stiff fight behind them, the 26th Division prepared to spend it's second and last monsoon in the Arakan. With it's companion the 25th Indian Division responsible for the bulk of the monsoon line, the " Tiger Heads " assumed a limited responsibility for the old bastions at Taung and Goppe and held a force back in reserve in the coastal plain, while one brigade was allowed to go for rest—though no further north than Cox's Bazar.

In the Goppe area the situation had much improved. A road had been engineered by 15 Corps sappers replacing the old mule track, and a ropeway—the first in Burma—had been built to supplement this line of communication which was still subject to interruption by landslides caused by monsoon storms. This new lifeline was a great sapper achievement, and pioneers and sapper detachments worked on it through the rain stripped to the waist keeping it open for traffic.

Even the brigade at Cox's had limited operational responsibilities, for there was all the eastern flank of the 15 Corps front still to be watched.

Still in command was General Lomax, admired by his men, a fine soldier and a stern disciplinarian. In April '44 on the first anniversary of his command, officers and men of the Division had presented him with a caravan built in the Division's own workshops in the field.

THE RIGHT ANSWER TO JAPANESE INFILTRATION.

General Lomax was no man to waste time. Even in the monsoon months his men were still training—back to weapon training, study of Japanese tactics, sports and games where intermittent sunshine permitted, to keep them fit, and co-operation courses between gunners and infantry. How fruitful was that training was shown in their later performance in battle.

But in the mind of the Jap commanders was still apparently a determination to get quits with the " Tiger Head " Division which had torn them so badly in past engagements.

No sooner had the monsoon rains come to an end, than the Jap with strange stubborness once more tried his right hook up the valley of the Kalapanzin.

It was not mistakenly that the incipient threat to the Goppe Pass had been appreciated, and garrisons maintained there to guard the approach to the Arakan coastal plain.

In early October, a Japanese task force, a mixed battalion strong swept up on to Taung Bazar in the early hours of the morning. They aimed once more to get astride the Goppe pass. One small force struck north where it bumped a battalion of the 9th Jats and our own irregulars, and paid a heavy price. The remainder were mauled by the Green Howards in their first action—and the Garhwalis, and by Indian mountain gunners and infantry mortars. They were poor inexperienced troops, their officers killed, they lost their heads. Some of our accurate mortaring is believed to have wiped out an officer recce party and chopped the head off the raiding force leaving it leaderless and inept. The force lost a quarter of its strength in casualties and broke up and drifted back down the Kalapanzin.

*   *   *   *

IN THE ARAKAN

THE ROAD TO BUTHIDAUNG *typical of the few and difficult roads which became the "life lines" of the Arakan.*

ARAKAN HILL COUNTRY. The picturesque but extremely difficult terrain through which the Division battled to victory.

NGAKYEDAUK PASS (Okeydoke Pass to 26 DIV.) showing one of the many bends in its tortuous length.

FROM THE TOP OF NGAKYEDAUK PASS a tank of the 25th Dragoons fires at Japanese in camouflaged positions on Hill 1070.

AN OBSERVER watches shells bursting on Hill 1070.

RAJPUTS hack out path on the side of Hill 551.

THE CAPTURE of the shell-blasted summit of Hill 551 gave the Division control of the Maungdaw-Buthidaung Road.

GOPPE PASS. The road as seen by a Don R. twisting and turning among narrow defiles.

BRITISH TROOPS search a dead Japanese in the Goppe area.

INDIAN TROOPS hunt out enemy stragglers near Goppe Bazar.

BENGAL and MADRAS SAPPERS and MINERS repair bomb damage on Ngakyedauk Pass road.

KYAUKPYU

Part II—Ramree, Letpan, Taungup.

THE AUTUMN came on and the "Tiger Head" Division was ready for a new and vital role in the Burma campaign—a decisive role. With its Arakan partner the 25th Indian Division and the 82nd West African Division—new recruit to the Arakan battlefield—it prepared for that swift series of leapfrog landings down the coast which was to clinch the issue in the Arakan, give us the long sought prize of Akyab port, and take the forces of 15 Corps half way down the west coast of Burma in three months.

25th Indian Division led off with its landings at Akyab and on the Myebon peninsula. Nine days after Myebon, on 21st January, 26th Indian Division made a bold leap on to the next stepping stone—Ramree Island—a large island with an excellent harbour and much needed room for airfields, ninety-bomber-minutes from both Rangoon and Mandalay.

After two brief skirmishes with Jap patrols, Kyaukpyu—the port of Ramree island and our landing point—was in our hands. A fierce naval bombardment by cruisers, destroyers and sloops, and bombing and strafing by Liberators, Mitchells and Thunderbolts five minutes before the first wave of assault boats was due to touch down, wiped out initial opposition on the beach itself.

RAMREE ISLAND. *Following a fierce naval and air bombardment the beaches*

of the defences, Indian troops of 26th Division force their way up and inland.

Within twelve hours of the Division's landing, the Japs were in full retreat.

By the third day, the Lincolns had reached Minbin, twenty miles from Kyaukpyu. By the end of the first week, sniped at almost continually by the retreating Jap, the men of 26th Division had cleared about two hundred square miles of Ramree—roughly the northern half of the island.

In eighteen days the forwardmost troops—the 1st Punjabs and the Lincolns—had marched seventy miles. It was an advance made possible by the heroic work of the Indian Sappers, who, working night after night by moonlight, cleared the large numbers of mine and booby traps left by the retreating enemy. In 18 working days and nights the Division's sappers built fifty miles of roads, repaired forty bridges, and cleared a number of airstrips.

As our troops entered Ramree Town, the Japs filtered away towards the maze of chaungs and mangrove swamps that fill the north-east corner of the island. But the Joint Assault Force Commander had anticipated this move. When the Japs tried to make their getaway by sampan from the mangroves to the mainland opposite, they found a reception party of the Royal Navy and the Arakan Coastal Force to greet them. Such was the slaughter inflicted in the days that followed by these naval " chaung-blocking " forces that dozens of floating corpses became a familiar feature of the creeks.

But Ramree is a big island—sixty miles long. Months after the landing, through the weeks when one of its brigades had left to forge forward to Taungup, until the time came to move on to Rangoon, 26th Division troops on Ramree were kept busy combing out and rounding up odd remnants of the Japs' Ramree garrison. Meanwhile Royal Navy Force " Wellington " had occupied Cheduba—a smaller island to the south of Ramree—which was taken over by troops of 26th Division very shortly after its capture.

While the mopping-up on Ramree had been going steadily on, the 26th's Arakan partner, the 25th Indian Division, had not been standing still. The Japs had been broken with great slaughter at Kangaw, their miserable remnants sent scattering through the mountains towards An. On the 15th February, the 25th took another southward leap landing at Ru-Ywa, on obscure Arakanese coastal village about 40 miles south of Myebon. From Ru-Ywa they thrust out north and East to Tamandu and towards An whence a track leads across the Arakan Yomas to Minbu.

Now it was the turn of the 26th again. 40 miles south of Ru-Ywa, the Taungup road ferries across the narrow Mai Chaung near the village of Pyin-wan. This point, reached by a maze of chaungs and mangrove swamps, was the place selected for the 26th's new strike.

The key task of the operation was entrusted to the 15th Frontier Force Rifles. The night before D-day they were to

PATROLLING IN A MAZE OF MANGROVE SWAMPS

land, make their way across country to Hill 1120 and take possession of it at all costs. This hill was necessary to safeguard the approach to the main beach.

Another pre-H-hour job was carried out by the 18th Garhwalis. With the Sappers they landed during the night before D-day to prepare for the unloading of guns so that medium field artillery could go into action at the earliest possible moment protecting the landing craft convoys as they came through.

Once again the Japs were taken utterly by surprise. This swift alternation of hammer blows by the twin divisions of the Arakan was too much for their Intelligence services. Documents later captured by us showed that the Jap Commander-in-Chief's office was often as much as a couple of weeks behind events—issuing streams of orders about the holding of positions which no longer existed.

By noon on D-day, endless streams of landing craft were surging up and down the chaung bearing reinforcements, vehicles and supplies.

In the first ten days after this new landing, our forces drove 23 miles southwards along the tortuous, coast road, and reached Tanlwe chaung, eleven miles from Taungup and the last water crossing before Taungup chaung itself.

An incident of these early days was the capture of five Jap tankettes—two of them intact—in a trap sprung by men of the 13th Frontier Force Rifles and 7th Rajput Regiment, reinforced by Grant tanks of 146th regiment of the Royal Armoured Corps.

The Frontier Force men spotted the Jap Tankettes advancing swiftly down the road towards them. They let them through without interference and immediately went to work to construct a road block behind them.

Five miles further down the road the Jap tankettes ran into the follow-up battalion of the Rajput Regiment—and the Grants.

Jungle-covered hills rise steeply on either side of the narrow winding track. As the Rajputs drove forward the crews of the Jap tankettes saw that they were trapped. They leaped out and made a dash for the jungle. Three of their tankettes they managed to set on fire. But the other two, the victors carried away in triumph.

Though in the earlier stages of the advance, opposition was very slight it was necessary to move forward with considerable caution because this was a " one brigade show "— and the brigade was becoming greatly extended along the coast. A break-through by the Japs suddenly marshalling in the hills that bordered the road was always a possibility that had to be reckoned with.

As Taungup was neared, Jap resistence began to stiffen. Delaying actions fought around blocks on the narrow road became fiercer. At the end of March '45 Major-General H. M. Chambers relieved Major-General C. E. N. Lomax as commander of the Division.

At one point the Japs had felled trees across the track for several hundred yards and were deeply entrenched with machine guns in the steep hillside. A small force of the 7th Rajput Regiment was feeling its way round the back of the hill when suddenly a Jap captain, waving a sword in his right hand and gripping a pistol in his left, leapt from a trench and ran at the company commander.

Lance-Naik Bishram Singh turned his Sten gun on the officer but it jammed. The captain raised his sword to strike the Rajput officer but before he could do so his wrist had been grabbed by Bishram Singh who in a lightning action seized the man's pistol and fired at him.

As the Jap fell dead three more ran up with fixed bayonets. Bishram Singh took the pin from a grenade, ducked behind a tree, threw the grenade—and killed the lot.

Almost within sight of Taungup the Japs put in a series of fierce counter-attacks on Hill 370—a steep jungle-covered position commanding the road. Eventually they succeeded in forcing our troops to withdraw but were speedily and finally dealt with by a Sikh company of the Frontier Force Rifles —in a forty-minutes battle, a little masterpiece of co-operation between infantry, tanks, mortars and machine-guns.

For many days past, as the cautious mopping-up of the brigade's flanks proceeded, every man had been itching to get on and into Taungup which—it was not quite another Mandalay—was nevertheless still something of a name to conjure with.

Then the news came. The 13/14th April was to be the night..a strong fighting patrol of the 7th Rajput Regiment forced Taungup chaung in the darkness, and penetrated into Taungup. Not a shot was fired.

Sole inhabitant of that town was the caretaker of the Government bungalow, an Orissa man named Manglu. He answered the patrol's knock on his door at 4 a.m. in the morning, and brought his guests' Register from its hiding place under the chicken coop for the Rajput leaders to sign. The last entry in the book had been made by a British officer in February 1942.

But though Taungup was empty, it was dominated by Jap artillery on a hill to the south-east. Until this and the surrounding hills had been cleared up, Taungup must still remain " No-Man's Land."

While the Rajputs were cautiously exploring Taungup itself—a nightly Jap patrol had left only half an hour before their arrival—a party of the Frontier Force Rifles had the supporting role of combing through the belt of villages that ring the town and steamer jetty. They encountered odd snipers and a few parties of Japs. These were duly plastered by our artillery.

From Taungup, an Indian Army observer wrote: "For these Arakan veterans of the 26th Indian Division this was the end of a long road—a road along which they have footslogged through monsoon mud and cruel jungle for two weary gruelling years."

But there was to be no rest yet. The brigade which had reached Taungup—a hundred miles or more further south than any other troops in Burma at that time, was now ordered not to drive the enemy any further, but to hand over to the 82nd West Africans and return with all speed to Ramree island.

PUNJABIS GOING ASHORE ON RAMREE ISLAND.

COMBINED OPERATIONS

KYAUKPYU BEACH. Indian Troops cross the beach and make their way inland.

ROYAL GARHWAL RIFLES attack Japanese position in Ramree mangrove swamps.

R.I.N. SLOOP lying in a chaung with her guns covering an enemy supply road between Myebon and Kyanla Pegu.

LETPAN. The second wave of landing craft goes in to reinforce those already landed.

L.C.M's of R.I.N. Landing Craft Wing putting supplies ashore on Letpan Beach.

TAUNGUP. British tank drives along the road from Letpan.

Captured enemy bullock carts used to bring up rations.

TAUNGUP. Men of the Rajput Regt. on the last lap of the road.

The Frontier Force Rifles battle on towards Taungup.

TAUNGUP. The 7th Rajput Regt. reach the end of the drive on the town which began at Letpan.

THE SHWE DAGON, RANGOON

Part III—Rangoon.

THE MEN of the 26th Indian Division were now to be given the biggest job of their career—a job of which every other division might envy them. They were to invade Rangoon from the sea—the expedition the world had so long been waiting for.

There was need for great haste: little time to plan. Indeed experts had given it as their opinion that the minimum time to plan such an expedition would be something very much longer than was in fact now possible. But 26th Indian Division were by this time past masters at planning " combined ops." Within sound of the surf on Ramree island, behind the barbed wire barricades of the planning camp, the officers of all three services swiftly got down to work.

It was clearly from the start, an enterprise fraught with many perils. Because of the shallow waters of the Irrawaddy estuary, not only would the expedition be deprived of the support of big naval guns, but the assault craft run-in would be the longest ever attempted in the whole course of amphibious warfare—nearly thirty miles.

The season was already advanced beyond the time previously considered safe for amphibious expeditions in these waters. A major invasion was being launched on the very verge of the monsoon. An early break might bring disaster to the whole enterprise.

The river over which the assault boats would have to travel for ten miles was sown with a three-year-old accumulation of mines—our own and Japanese.

Perhaps the most formidable risk of the lot—the Jap guns on " Elephant Point "—" Gibraltar " of Rangoon at the mouth of the the river : Gurkha paratroops were being dropped to deal with these on D-Day-minus 1. But because of the radio silence the invasion armada would not know whether they had been successful till they were about to enter the river. Consequently alternative plans had to be made so that, if those guns were still firing, the Japs could not have worked terrible destruction among the defenceless landing craft as they filed past the point.

But the risks were measured—and the risks were taken.

Shortly after 7 o'clock on the morning of 2nd May, seasick, drenched to the skin, stiff from six hours crouching in the bellies of their little assault boats, men of the 9th Jats, 13th Frontier Force Rifles, 8th Gurkhas, Lincolns, 1st Punjab and Garhwalis with their British gunners, tanks and other supporting arms ran up the soggy beaches on both sides of the Rangoon river—ten miles below Rangoon.

The Japs, locals told our men, had left some days before. The only casualty of the actual landing was one man, gored by a bull, although in the later stages casualties occurred owing to sea mines and during the round-up of small parties of Japanese ' die hards '.

Next day, while a Punjabi armoured column struck out for Syriam, oil refinery town across the river from Rangoon— Frontier Force, Jats, Gurkhas and Garhwalis, piled back on to their landing craft, and, sailing past bombtorn quaysides thronged with cheering townspeople, in pouring rain, made a fresh assault landing into Burma's capital.

The Divisional Commander went straight to the gaol to see the six hundred British, Indian, Chinese and Dominion prisoners who had been dreaming, many of them for years, of this moment. Many of the prisoners were ill and emaciated. Immediate arrangements were made to get them aboard ship and on their way back to India without a day's delay.

Right from the moment the expedition sailed from Kyaukpyu, the men of the 26th Indian Division had been asking each other whether they would not arrive in Rangoon to find the 14th Army already there to greet them. Such was the pace of the 14th's progress down the Central Burma plain that General Leese himself, briefing war correspondents, had given the odds heavily in favour of General Slim's men.

Now the 26th were " in "—and they had found in themselves the first representatives of the United Nations to return to this earliest of Britain's great Imperial capitals to be liberated.

But the question still being asked, every hour of the day, was: " Where is the Fourteenth Army ? ". Two days after the landing there was still no communication between the two forces.

Patrols were pushed out northwards through the outskirts of the city. Save for a few stragglers here and there, no Japs were encountered. In Rangoon itself, some thousands of Indian National Army men waited at their depot to be disarmed—setting a new sort of problem to army commanders.

Then came the news that the advance body of the 14th Army had reached the village of Hlegu on the Pegu road north of Rangoon where they were held up by a broken bridge and where a column from 26th Division linked up with them.

Sixty miles north of Rangoon another meeting of tank columns, one from the 20th Indian Division which had fought its way down Burma on the Prome road, the other from the 26th Indian Division which had entered Rangoon via the Arakan and the front door, marked the beginning of a new stage in the liberation of South East Asia. Neither route had been easy.

The G.O.C. of the 26th Indian Division assumed the Military Governorship of Rangoon area—allotting to each of his brigades an area of the city to administer and restore to order. The Division's specialist troops lent all the aid they could towards getting the life of the town running smoothly again. The Sappers and Miners found themselves wrestling with five-ton fractured water pipes, restoring the city's water supply. The medical officers of the Division's No. 1 Field Ambulance confronted a new sort of sick parade—an ever lengthening queue of Burmese, Chinese and Indians who had not been able to get medical treatment under the Japs.

The 26th had hit the jackpot. They were in Rangoon—where for so many weary months the men of every Division in Burma had vaguely dreamed of one day being. But if the reward was an impressive one—so was the 26th's total of undrawn credits. It was in fact rather in the line of poetic justice—a not unfitting recompense for the two gruelling years of obscurity in the Arakan where, though well out of the play of the limelight, the Division had been doing an indispensable job in disrupting Jap supply lines and building up the air and sea communications necessary to nourish the main body of South East Asia Forces fighting their way down the interior of Burma.

INTO RANGOON

THE WAY INTO RANGOON. Smoke from fires started by aircraft marks the point where troops will land.

THE FINAL APPROACH. The first Landing craft pass the jetties in Rangoon River prior to disembarkation.

BENGAL SAPPERS and MINERS work on new water main to supply Rangoon.

RANGOON. Gurkha troops marching through the liberated city.

RANGOON DOCKS. The battered warehouses and quayside buildings bear testimony to the accuracy of our bombing.

VICTORY DAY RANGOON. The Supreme Allied Commander takes the salute as troops of the Division march past.

PEACE IN RANGOON
The end of the long and arduous journey
for the 26th INDIAN DIVISION.

INDIAN DIVISIONS WON A FINE REPUTATION IN WORLD WAR TWO

Field Marshal Auchinleck, Commander-in-Chief of the British Indian Army from 1942, asserted that the British *"couldn't have come through both wars (World War I and II) if they hadn't had the British Indian Army"*. British Prime Minister Winston Churchill also paid tribute to *"the unsurpassed bravery of Indian soldiers and officers"*.

Between 1945 and 1947, the Director of Public Relations, War Department, Government of India, published a series of short publications covering the individual histories of the WWII Indian Divisions. They followed a consistent format, having between 44 and 48 pages within illustrated soft card covers. They have an average of 50 monochrome photographic illustrations, and each has a full colour centrespread depicting a scene from the Division's wartime operations (drawn by official war artists). They were printed at various presses in Bombay and New Delhi, and each contains at least one map.

As condensed histories they are useful – particularly those which relate to Divisions for which no other record was ever produced.

The British Indian Army during World War II began the war, in 1939, numbering just under 200,000 men. By the end of the war, it had become the largest volunteer army in history, rising to over 2.5 million men in August 1945. Serving in divisions of infantry, armour and a fledgling airborne force, they fought on three continents: in Africa, Europe and Asia.

This Army fought in Ethiopia against the Italian Army, in Egypt, Libya, Tunisia and Algeria against both the Italian and German Army and, after the Italian surrender, against the German Army in Italy. However, the bulk of the British Indian Army was committed to fighting the Japanese Army, first during the British defeats in Malaya and the retreat from Burma to the Indian border; later, after resting and refitting for the victorious advance back into Burma, as part of the largest British Empire army ever formed. These campaigns cost the lives of over 87,000 Indian service- men, while another 34,354 were wounded, and 67,340 became prisoners of war. Their valour was recognised with the award of some 4,000 decorations, and 18 members of the British Indian Army were awarded the Victoria Cross or the George Cross.

RED EAGLES
The Story of the 4th Indian Division
9781474537520

During the Second World War, the 4th Indian Division was in the vanguard of nine campaigns in the Mediterranean theatre, Egypt, Eritrea, Syria, Tunisia, Italy and Greece. The 4th Division captured 150,000 prisoners and suffered 25,000 casualties, more than the strength of a whole division. It won over 1,000 honours and awards, which included four Victoria Crosses and three George Crosses. Field Marshal Lord Wavell wrote: "The fame of this Division will surely go down as one of the greatest fighting formations in military history."

THE FIGHTING FIFTH
History of the 5th Indian Division
9781474537513

As described in much greater detail in Anthony Brett James's book 'The Ball of Fire', the division saw active service in East Africa, North Africa and Burma.

GOLDEN ARROW
The Story of the 7th Indian Division
9781474537506

The role of this division is also duplicated by a much larger work: the book by Brig. M. R. Roberts. However, this booklet gives a good account of Kohima and Imphal and the crossing of the Irrawaddy. In 1945, the division was flown into Siam, so becoming the first Allied formation to re-enter South East Asia.

ONE MORE RIVER
The Story of the 8th Indian Division
Biferno, Trigno, Sangro, Moro, Rapido, Arno, Senio, Santerno, Po, Adige

9781474537490

The 8th Indian Division started its overseas service in the Middle East in the garrisoning of Iraq and then the invasion of Persia to secure the oil fields of the area for the Allies, before moving to Italy in 1943. Landing at Taranto, it pushed up the length of the peninsula in a series of major battles: breaking the Sangro Line, forcing the Rapido and turning the defences at Cassino, breaking the stubborn German resistance at Monte Grande and, finally, forcing the Po River. It won four VCs, 26 DSOs and 149 MCs along the way. During the war the 8th Indian Division sustained casualties totalling 2,012 dead, 8,189 wounded and 749 missing.

BLACK CAT DIVISION
17th Indian Division

9781474537483

This formation was committed to Burma from the early days when the British were in full flight from the invading Japanese. It remained in Burma right through to the end, when the starving remnants of the Japanese Army were making their own desperate retreat.

TIGER HEAD
The Story of the 26th Indian Division
Arakan, Ragoon

9781474537452

This is a history of the division said later by the Japanese to have been the opponent which they most feared. The 26th held the Allied monsoon line in the Arakan during two such seasons, repulsing every attack launched against it. Later it made a series of leap-frog landings down the coast to clinch the issue in the Arakan. It was the first division to enter Ragoon, invading the city from the sea.

A HAPPY FAMILY
The Story of the Twentieth Indian Division, April 1942-August 1945

9781474537476

One of the few Indian divisions in the 14th Army trained specifically for the war in Burma. Raised in Bangalore in 1942, it commenced active operations in late 1943 and served from Imphal through to the end. It established the 14th Army's first brigade-head across the Chindwin and its second such brigade-head across the Irrawaddy. Its final task was to round up the Japanese in French Indochina.

THE TWENTY THIRD INDIAN DIVISION
"The Fighting Cock Division"
Burma, Malaya, Java

9781474537469

The Fighting Cock Division is well recorded in the book by Doulton. This book gives coverage of the heavy fighting at the Kohima Battle, the capture of Tamu, the reoccupation of Malaya in August 1945, and then its strange role on the island of Java – concurrently disarming the Japanese garrison, fighting the insurgent Indonesian nationalists, and caring for 65,000 former internees pending the arrival of a new Dutch administration.

TEHERAN TO TRIESTE
The Story Of The Tenth Indian Division

9781783317028

This History deals with the 10th Indian Div's exploits in Iraq (under Maj Gen "Bill" Slim) its role in the Libyan battles leading up to El Alamein, the following two years of garrison duties in Cyprus and Syria, and finally, its fighting services in the Italian campaign (from Ortona onwards).

THE STORY OF THE 25th INDIAN DIVSION
The Arakan Campaign
9781783317585

Formed in Southern India in August 1942 for defence of that area in case of Japanese invasion, the "Ace of Spades" Division had its baptism of fire in Arakan in February 1944. It served throughout the remainder of that campaign the climax being the battle of Tamandu. Its victorious fight for the Kangaw roadblock was considered by many to have been the fiercest battle of the entire Burma war, while its liberation of Akyab was the first convincing proof to the rest of the world that the tide had turned against the Japanese.

DAGGER DIVISION
The Story Of The 19th Indian Division
9781783317035

Raised in the late 1941, the 19th was the first "standard" Indian Division. Its troops were the first to breach the Japanese defence line in Burma and to raise the flag at Fort Dufferin. It crossed the Chindwin in November 1944, driving on to Mandalay and Ragoon during seven months of continuous fighting. The 19th's exploits are graphically described also in John Masters' personal memoir, *The Road Past Mandalay*.

www.ingramcontent.com/pod-product-compliance
Lightning Source LLC
Chambersburg PA
CBHW041928090426
42743CB00021B/3475